How To Study The Bible From 5 To 1

Student Workbook

How To Study The Bible From 5 To 1

Student Workbook

Keithron D. Powell

ISBN 978-1-105-59688-9

This book was printed in the United States of America.

All scripture quotation is from the King James Version (KJV) version of the Bible. Public Domain.

How to Study the Bible from 5 To 1

Student Workbook

Table of Contents

This book is the companion workbook to
How To Study The Bible From 5 - 1

Section 1
Understanding Study
2 Tim 2:15

Study *to shew thyself approved unto God, a workman that needeth not to be ashamed, rightly dividing the word of truth.*

What is studying?

____

____

____

____

____

____

Explain each of these

1) Reading

____

____

____

____

____

____

____

____

____

2) Investigation

3) Reflection

What is the purpose of studying?

Where should you begin studying?

____
____
____
____
____
____

What do you want to gain from your study of the Bible?

____
____
____
____
____
____

Section 2

Define the underlined words and place them in the chart below.

2 Timothy 2:15

Study to shew thyself approved unto God, a workman that needeth not to be ashamed, rightly dividing the word of truth.

English	Greek	Definition

English	Greek	Definition

Using the literal definitions of those words reconstruct the verse.

2 Timothy 2:15

____

____

____

____

____

____

What does this definition reveal?

____

____

____

____

____

____

Section 3
TOOLS FOR STUDY

List the tools that you use for your Bible study.

____

____

____

____

____

____

BIBLE
What version of the Bible do you use?

____

Is the version of Bible important?

____

What do you know about how it was created?

____

____

____

____

____

____

Reference Material

What reference material do you use?

____
____
____
____
____
____

Do you verify the accuracy of the material you use?

____

Why or Why not?

____
____
____
____
____
____

Internet

Do you use the internet for your study?

____

Do you verify the information is accuracy before accepting it as such?

____

Do you think it is important to verify the information?

____

Define These Terms

Etymology:

____

____

____

____

____

____

Prayer

____

____

____

____

____

____

Meditation

____

____

____

____

____

____

Do you apply these terms to your study time?

______

Section 4

What is your motivation for studying the Bible?

____

____

____

____

____

____

Do you think your motivations hinder, help or have no affect at all on your study of the Bible?

____

____

____

____

____

____

Why do you want to know more about God?

____

____

____

____

____

____

Do you think you make any errors in your study?

List what you believe could be a potential error in your study.

1____
2____
3____
4____
5____
6____

John 14:26

But the Comforter which is the Holy Ghost, whom the Father will send in my name, he shall teach you all things and bring all things to your remembrance whatsoever I have said unto you.

In your own words explain this verse.

Section 5

The study method is based on 6 questions.

Who?
What?
Why?
When?
Where?
How?

Using Matthew 16:13-20 Answer the following questions

1. Who is talking?

____

2. What are they talking about?

____
____
____

3. What did he say?

____
____
____

4. What was the reply?

____
____
____

5. What was the end result?

6. What are the keys?

7. Who was given the keys?

8. What was the response of Peter?

9. Who provided Peter with the answer to the question?

10. Why did Jesus point out his name?

____

____

____

11. What is the meaning of his name?

____

12. What was Jesus building?

____

13. What is the meaning of Simon Barjona?

____

14. What was the rock that Jesus was going to build upon?

____

____

15. What is meant by the gates of hell not prevailing?

____

____

____

16. Why is binding and loosing so important?

____

____

____

17. Why advise the disciples that they shouldn't tell anyone who he was?

______

______

______

18. What does Christ mean?

______

19. Who is John the Baptist?

______

20. Who is Elias?

______

21. Who is Jeremias?

______

22. Who are the other prophets that the people referred to and what do we know about them?

______

______

______

______

______

______

23. How did the disciples get the answers to Jesus' question?

24. Why did Jesus even ask them this question?

25. What is the significance of Jesus referring to himself as "The Son of Man?"

26. Where is Caesarea Philippi?

27. What is the significance of Caesarea Philippi to the question that was asked?

28. What is the history of Caesarea Philippi?

29. What stands out about the answer that Peter gave?

30. Why did Jesus even ask them this question?

31. What stands out about the answer that Peter gave or was his answer unique in ANY way?

After answering these questions what stands out about this story that is different from what you may have initially thought?

____

____

____

____

____

____

Section 6

Biblical Interpretation

In any field of study there is typically a set of basic rules to follow to ensure that the outcome isn't tainted or inaccurate. Do you think this is or should be the case with Biblical study?

____

Explain

____

____

____

____

____

____

Below is a list of general Biblical Interpretation rules. Explain each rule and give an example to support your explanation.

Understand the Context of the Passage.

____

____

____

____

____

____

The Unexplainable is not necessarily Unexplainable

Interpret difficult passages considering clear ones

Don't base teachings on obscure passages

Just because a report is incomplete does not mean it is incorrect or false

____

____

____

____

____

____

New Testament citations of the Old Testament need not always be exact

____

____

____

____

____

____

The Bible does not necessarily approve of all it records

____

____

____

____

____

____

Later revelation supersedes previous revelation

Scripture Interprets Scripture

Define words even when you think you know the meaning

26

Never apply an Old Testament passage to your life without first filtering it through the Cross of Calvary

____

____

____

____

____

____

Contact Pastor Keithron Powell

Pastor Keithron Powell
Victory In Praise Outreach Ministries, Jacksonville, FL

Email Keithron D. Powell
pastorkeith@vipomonline.com

Visit our website
www.vipomonline.com

www.facebook.com/keithronp

More Exciting Titles
By Pastor Keithron Powell

In this book Pastor Keithron Powell explains the 3 major phases of study Reading, Investigation and Reflection. In the end you will apply his easy 5 to 1 method to Matthew 16:13-19 and then begin using it in your very own personal study.

Available at www.lulu.com

Trial of a Father and Son is a practical look at apologetics and theology. Witness the trial of Pastor Miller as he expounds the scripture in court, in front of a jury of people that are not quite his peers, answering some of Christianity's most difficult questions.

ISBN: 978-1-4415-8661-2

Available online at Barnes and Noble and Amazon.

33

Pastor Keithron Powell cleverly brings the experience of Social Media to written form. This book is spiritual, practical and funny. And it doesn't even matter if you start at the beginning of the book or not. This is the book you carry with you when you can't have your iPhone.

Available at www.lulu.com

Suggested Reading By Pastor Keithron Powell

"Preparing An Atmosphere for True Worship" is a must have for every believer. Discover how worship goes beyond the four walls of the church and how you can "Make Worship Count" in this exciting and insightful book by Teresa G. Powell.

ISBN:978-1-4500-2827-1
Available online at Amazon and Barnes and Noble.

www.ingramcontent.com/pod-product-compliance
Ingram Content Group UK Ltd.
Pitfield, Milton Keynes, MK11 3LW, UK
UKHW041902190726
13854UKWH00003B/1041

9 781105 596889